# Life in the Past

## Victorian Homes

**Mandy Ross**

**Heinemann**
**LIBRARY**

www.heinemann.co.uk/library
Visit our website to find out more information about **Heinemann Library** books.

To order:

☎ Phone ++44 (0)1865 888066
▤ Send a fax to ++44 (0)1865 314091
▣ Visit the Heinemann Bookshop at *www.heinemann.co.uk/library* to browse our catalogue
and order online.

First published in Great Britain by Heinemann Library, Halley Court, Jordan Hill, Oxford OX2 8EJ, part of Harcourt Education. Heinemann is a registered trademark of Harcourt Education Ltd.

Editorial: Lucy Thunder and Helen Cannons
Design: Ron Kamen and Paul Davies
Picture Research: Rebecca Sodergren and Liz Savery
Production: Edward Moore
Originated by Repro Multi-Warna
Printed and bound in Hong Kong and China by South China Printing Company
The paper used to print this book comes from sustainable resources.

ISBN 0 431 12141 9       ISBN 0 431 12146 X
(hardback)               (paperback)
08 07 06 05 04           09 08 07 06 05
10 9 8 7 6 5 4 3 2 1     10 9 8 7 6 5 4 3 2 1

**British Library Cataloguing in Publication Data**

Ross, Mandy
Victorian homes. – (Life in the past)
640.9'41'09034

A full catalogue record for this book is available from the British Library.

**Acknowledgements**
The Publishers are grateful to the following for permission to reproduce photographs:
Bridgeman Art Library/Guildhall, Corporation of London, UK p26; Bridgeman Art Library/The International Fine Art Auctioneers, UK p25; Bridgeman Art Library/Private Collection pp5, **13**; Bridgeman Art Library/Walker Art Gallery, Liverpool, UK p**15**; Corbis p**7**; Corbis/Bettmann p**17**; Corbis/Hulton-Deutsch Collection p24; Fine Art Photographic Library Ltd/Private Collection p**8**; Hulton Archive pp**4**, **6**, **14**, **19**; Mary Evans Picture Library pp**9**, **12**, **18**, **20**, **22**, **23**; Museum of London p**16**; National Trust Photographic Library p**29**; Robert Opie pp**10**, **11**, **21**; Saltaire Village Society p**27**; Tudor Photography p**28**.

Cover photo of a washer woman and her son at home in 1891 reproduced with permission of Corbis/Bettman.

Our thanks to Jane Shuter for her assistance in the preparation of this book.

# Contents

Who were the Victorians? . . . . . . . . . . . 4

Homes then and now . . . . . . . . . . . . . . 6

Rich people's homes . . . . . . . . . . . . . . 8

Money to spend . . . . . . . . . . . . . . . . 10

The slums . . . . . . . . . . . . . . . . . . . 12

A pretty country cottage? . . . . . . . . . . 14

A woman's work is never done . . . . . . . 16

What is for dinner? . . . . . . . . . . . . . . 18

Where is the bathroom? . . . . . . . . . . . 20

Time for bed . . . . . . . . . . . . . . . . . . 22

Playing at home . . . . . . . . . . . . . . . . 24

Healthier homes . . . . . . . . . . . . . . . . 26

Let's find out! . . . . . . . . . . . . . . . . . 28

Timeline . . . . . . . . . . . . . . . . . . . . 30

Glossary . . . . . . . . . . . . . . . . . . . . 31

Find out more . . . . . . . . . . . . . . . . . 31

Index . . . . . . . . . . . . . . . . . . . . . . 32

Words written in bold, **like this**, are explained
in the Glossary.

# Who were the Victorians?

Queen Victoria **reigned** in Britain from 1837 to 1901. People who lived during this time are known as the Victorians. Queen Victoria lived a long life, and she had many grand homes.

This photograph shows Queen Victoria outside her castle at Balmoral, in Scotland.

Queen Victoria

👆 These poor people's homes are right beside a dirty, dangerous factory.

Some Victorians were very rich – but many were poor. During Victoria's reign, new factories made all kinds of modern **inventions**. But factory workers lived in crowded homes, and worked very long hours.

5

# Homes then and now

Life in Victorian homes was very different from today. Most homes had no taps with running water, or electricity for light or heat. Homes were heated by lighting a fire in the fireplace.

This photograph shows a Victorian home with grand furnishings.

candles for light

These children are baking in a modern kitchen.

Electricity, running water and modern heating make today's homes more comfortable and easier to run. How many things in your home use electricity?

# Rich people's homes

Rich people lived in very large homes with many rooms. They needed lots of **servants** to do all the hard work. Most rich women never worked.

Katherine Mansfield, a writer, hated this kind of life:

'The days full of parties, the hours full of talking about clothes, the waste of life.'

servant

Servants cooking in the kitchen of a grand house.

Servants worked long hours for very little pay. They cooked, served grand meals, cleaned and lit fires to keep the house warm. They often shared small bedrooms, high in the attic.

# Money to spend

Many **middle-class** families lived in quite large houses. They could afford to make their homes comfortable. Advertisements encouraged people to buy new **inventions**.

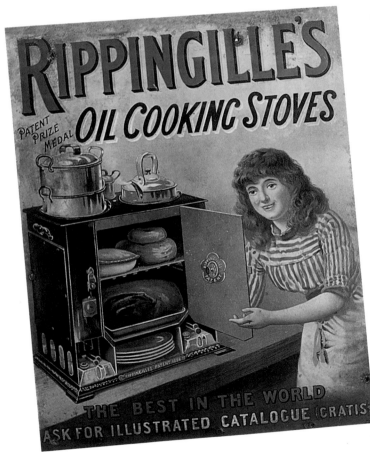

A Victorian advertisement for a new stove, which used oil instead of coal.

This advert for lamp oil shows children in a middle-class home. ☞

"'Tis so Light, Mamma We thought it was Time to get up."

"WHITE ROSE" LAMP OIL.

Most homes did not have electric lights until after the end of Victoria's **reign**. Instead they were lit by candles, **oil** lamps or gas lamps. Victorian homes would seem dark and gloomy to us.

# The slums

During Victoria's **reign**, people moved to towns to work in the new factories. Workers' houses were often badly built and cramped. Many people lived in dreadful conditions in the **slums**.

This worker's house in London belongs to a large family. The house is very dirty.

Several families shared a water pump, which gave out dirty water. Many children died from diseases which are easy to cure today.

water pump

# A pretty country cottage?

For some, life in the countryside was hard. Many farmworkers' homes went with their jobs. If they lost their job, they had to leave the house that went with it.

Life would have been cold and damp in this stone house in Scotland.

 This Victorian painting shows a good meal on the table for these country children.

Other families were more comfortable, though. At least in the countryside there might be room outdoors to keep a cow or hens to give milk and eggs.

# A woman's work is never done

Housework was hard work, whether it was done by servants or by women in poorer families. There were no electric machines to help, such as electric irons, washing machines or vacuum cleaners.

A Victorian flat iron had to be heated again and again on the fire. This washing day song explains the boring work.

'Oh, the weary, weary washing day.
We rub, rub, rub, on each washing day;
We scrub, scrub, scrub all our strength away ...'

Washing was hot, heavy work for women. Water was heated on a stove, and clothes scrubbed by hand on a **washing board**.

This woman is washing her clothes by hand in a washing tub. 👉

washing tub

washing board

# What is for dinner?

Rich families ate huge meals with many courses. Children were expected to behave very well at mealtimes.

This poem explains some of the rules for Victorian children:

A child should always say what's true,
And speak when he is spoken to,
And behave mannerly at table;
At least as far as he is able.
by *Robert Louis Stevenson*

Poorer families might only have one pan to cook in. They ate simple food. Sometimes a meal was just bread with a cup of tea. Many people often went hungry.

 This photograph shows a family at the table in a poorer home.

# Where is the bathroom?

Few homes had bathrooms or taps with running water. Instead, water was heated and poured into a tin tub for a bath, often in front of the fire.

 Washing a little boy in the tub.

Most poor families had to share a toilet outdoors. But rich Victorian families might have a **water closet** or flushing toilet – a new **invention**. This was a great luxury.

This advertisement is for a flushing water closet. ☞

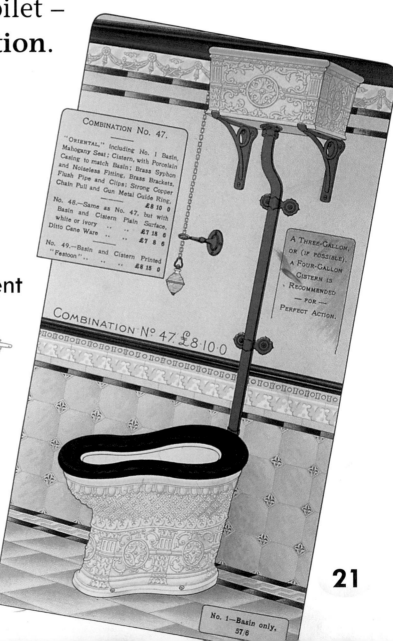

COMBINATION No. 47.

"ORIENTAL," including No. 1 Basin, Mahogany Seat; Cistern, with Porcelain Casing to match Basin; Brass Syphon and Noiseless Fitting, Brass Brackets, Flush Pipe and Clips; Strong Copper Chain Pull and Gun Metal Guide Ring.

£8 10 0

No. 48.—Same as No. 47, but with Basin and Cistern Plain Surface, white or ivory .. .. £7 18 6
Ditto Cane Ware .. .. £7 8 6

No. 49.—Basin and Cistern Printed "Festoon" .. .. £8 15 0

A THREE-GALLON, OR (IF POSSIBLE), A FOUR-GALLON CISTERN IS RECOMMENDED — FOR — PERFECT ACTION.

COMBINATION No. 47. £8.10.0

No. 1—Basin only, 57/6

Children in well-off families wore clean cotton nightgowns and slept in comfortable beds. They might have had a **copper** warming pan filled with hot water to warm the bed.

These two children are saying their prayers at bedtime. They are wearing clean cotton nightgowns. ☞

In poorer families several children shared a bed. In winter it was very cold. Poor children had no warming pans to keep the bed warm.

A Victorian girl remembers the cold nights:

'We took off only our boots and jumped into bed fully clothed. The three of us huddled together to keep warm, with the grey blanket and coats over us.'

# Playing at home

The Victorians had no television or computer games. Children in poorer families had few toys. They played together outside in the street or the fields. There was no room to play indoors.

These children are chatting together while they play outdoors.

Children in rich families had more toys, but many saw little of their parents. **Middle-class** families spent time together at home, reading aloud or singing together.

👉 This painting shows children dancing while their mother plays the piano.

# Healthier homes

Victorian cities were full of dirt and disease. **Scientists** discovered that drinking dirty water caused disease. **City councils** started to build **sewers** to keep dirty water away from drinking water.

☝ Digging a sewer in a London street in 1845.

New **laws** in 1875 meant that some of the worst **slum** houses had to be cleared. This made way for better, healthier homes. Some factory owners built good housing for their workers.

New towns and villages were built especially for factory workers. This village, called Saltaire, in Yorkshire was built from 1850 to 1870.

# Let's find out

Today, many people live in houses built in Victorian times. Streets look different now, though. Roads are paved and cars are parked on the streets.

These Victorian houses are over 100 years old, but people still live in them today.

☞ Modern children visiting the kitchen in a big Victorian house.

Can you spot any Victorian buildings in your area? Some grand Victorian homes are now open to the public. Your local museum or library will have information about life in Victorian times, and places to visit.

# Timeline

1834 Poor **Law** sets out harsh treatment for poor or homeless people

1837 Victoria crowned Queen of Great Britain

1851 The Great Exhibition at the Crystal Palace, London. Many new **inventions** for the home are on display.

1853 Sir Titus Salt opens Saltaire, a small town in northern England with good quality homes for workers in his woollen mill

1854 British troops fight in the Crimean War against Russia

1861 Prince Albert, Victoria's husband, dies

1862 William Morris start to design wallpapers, furnishings and fabrics

1870 Dr Barnardo opens his first home for homeless children in London

1875 New laws start to make cities cleaner and to improve the poorest housing

1876 Alexander Graham Bell invents the telephone

1879 Thomas Edison invents the electric light

1888 Port Sunlight opens. It is a planned town with good housing for workers at the Lever brothers' soap factory near Liverpool.

1901 Queen Victoria dies

# Glossary

**city council** organization that runs a city

**copper** kind of orange metal

**invention** something made in a new way, or a new way of doing something

**law** rule made by parliament that everyone must obey

**middle-class** people who are fairly well-off and educated, such as doctors

**oil** kind of fuel used for lights, stoves and heating

**reign** to be the king or queen of a country, or the period a person spent ruling the country

**scientist** someone who studies nature and the world by testing and measuring

**servant** poorer person who lives and works in rich people's homes

**sewers** underground pipes which take away dirty water from toilets, bathrooms and kitchens

**slums** damp, unhealthy and overcrowded housing, with a water pump and a toilet shared between many families

**washing board** ribbed wooden board used to scrub washing

**water closet** another name for a flushing toilet

## Find out more

### More books to read

*Life in Victorian Britain: The Victorians at Home,* Rosemary Rees (Heinemann Library, 1995)

*Life in Victorian Times: Home and School,* Neil Morris (Belitha Press, 2000)

*People in the Past: Victorian Homes,* Brenda Williams (Heinemann Library, 2003)

### Places and websites to visit

*www.nationaltrust.org.uk*
The National Trust has information about historic buildings to visit in your area

*www.museumofchildhood.org.uk*
The Museum of Childhood in London has displays about many aspects of Victorian childhood.

# Index

baths  20
bedtime  22–3

castles  4
children  13, 18, 22,
    23, 24–5, 30
countryside  14–15

diseases  13, 26

electricity  6, 7, 11,
    16, 30

factory workers  5,
    12, 27, 30
farmworkers  14

heating  6
housework  16–17

inventions  5, 10,
    21, 30
irons  16

laws  27, 30
lighting  6, 11

meals  18, 19
middle-class families
    10, 11, 25
modern homes  7

playing  24–5
poor people  5, 12–13,
    19, 21, 23, 24

rich people  8, 18,
    22, 25

servants  8, 9, 16
sewers  26
slums  12, 27

toilets  21
toys  24, 25

Victoria, Queen  4, 30
Victorians  4, 5

washing clothes  16, 17
water  6, 13, 20, 26
water closets  21